AF260463

Somewhere Between Love and 3 AM

Kai Anderson

Copyright © 2023

All Rights Reserved

Contents

Dedication

For the love, I never wanted to lose.

The love I never thought I deserved.

To the lovers of my past and future.

And finally,

You, my reader, and all the ones you think about whilst reading each chapter.

For me

For you.

Acknowledgement

I want to thank my amazing team of editors, Natalia Adler and Heidi Adams, who supported me day and night to deliver this book beyond what I had imagined it. I also want to recognise all those who broke my heart before I had experienced the world; without you, these pages would not exist. I owe the most gratitude to S, my sweetest and most patient love. You collected all the emotions from these crumpled pages and pushed me to channel these experiences positively. Your love and belief in me have been glued into the bindings of this book. Some of these pages belong to you, my ode to you; we love you very much.

About the Author

When I was a child, I had always dreamed about writing a book. I wrote so many poems, stories and blogs about my life and all that I endured growing up. It was only twenty-four when survival mode turned into "I survived" I could take the time to write this book. Here you'll see through my eyes how I survived love and multiple complex failed relationships. Each chapter will take you with me to explore the darkest of days but also the bright optimism of "for ever after" My story doesn't begin here I have so much left unsaid to write, it also doesn't end here there is so much beauty unwritten like the birth of my daughter in 2019. I'd be naïve to think only I could experience love and heartbreak – this journey isn't just mine it's *OURS.*

Runaway Love

For all the love they had to

give,

but never to you.

<u>Coffee</u>

So delicate and simple

It gives the highest of buzzes and the deepest thoughts

It's a blank canvas and you, the drinker, are the artist

Placing my lips on your mocha skin for the very first time

The taste lingered

That sip warmed a cold soul from the inside out

Bitterness hides in a candid disguise

And you've always preferred tea

But not today...

No sugar in the raw

No milk

No cream

No sweet sticky flavours to trick my lovesick mind

No fancy name to make you think it's worth the cost

Just pure dark caffeine

Ground up this morning

Smooth, rich yet bitter and dry

Brewed with intention

Just a coffee kiss

For you,

And,

But…

You've always preferred tea.

My life on every page

I promise it's worth picking up

A few rips and crumpled-up pages

But it all adds character

You came along,

I convinced you to start reading this chapter

I'd been waiting my whole life for this

Then you decided I wasn't worth reading to the end

Suddenly my entire story fell apart.

Admire me from afar

Because when you get too close, you will leave me with scars

It's not intentional our forces cannot be aligned

You've got your power, I have mine

We're not meant for each other

I guess that's fine

I'll still love and care for you, but from far away

Even if I see you in another lifetime

Just know our souls still can't combine

What we have is special, but together would never work

It wasn't love, just a fairy-tale

A story with an end because…

Love never fails.

I don't write about love just to write about us

I write about love because I'm hoping to show someone how to trust

Open up,

Knowing this time, they will be enough

The same lesson I'll teach my daughters or unborn son

Cause at home is where you find the courage to love

From a young, our idea of love starts at home

And if we don't nurture it and let it grow,

Ultimately the harsh reality is exposed

My idea of love never came from home

It came from long days and late nights watching family shows,

Where uncle Phil and Aunt Viv welcomed any stray in

I walked into my first foster placement like the "fresh prince"

Everyone's grown up with separate love, so surely there's an idea it's all different

Yet we can look to our friends and tell them they're in it

How can it be that we all have the same perception

Cause what I thought was love, what you told me was love, turned out to be deception

The minutes that pass are timeless and the seconds last forever

And everything just seems to get worse just when it starts to get better

Self-sabotaging any relationship because this "love" thing's a setup

It must be I learned that from you.

I held onto you like September holds onto summer

Being patient with you while you fight demons

Working through things and trying to change

But sometimes,

Only sometimes,

Waiting for people like this

Is a waste of time,

While they lie and manipulate you

Doing nothing to change

I had to learn to stop seeing what you could've been

And see what you were and always will be.

I gave you so much of me; I don't regret it, either

I hope you keep these parts beside you

They could teach a few things, like how to love harder or stick
around

I would never take that back

My gifts will die with you

The reason they're not with me

I can't and don't want to be that person for you anymore

You know,

That person who became complacent

Happy to be second best

Ignoring red flags in hopes of better days

I put the batteries in my clock, and with time

I gave myself the power to move on

Left behind the part of me that loved you

Let it remind you of what you lost.

Although our love story never started

I'd still walk with you to the end of the world, then

Past it.

My fingernails broke from a bold attempt to bury the memories

Painful to remember that our love had an expiration date

I think about you in all I do

You're nothing but a ghost now

A close memory

I'm haunted by you

I keep thinking that it will be the last time

That I could really wash the bloodshed from this disaster

But instead, I remain

In a heap at the bottom of our shower

Hoping it'll all wash away.

I tried to teach you how to love me

Like the journey was yours to follow

You were dead weight I tried to drag to the finish line

In hope that you'd see my bleeding heart

You'd know I gave my all to take us to that place

But you dug your heels in

Added extra weight

You did everything you could to stop me

And when you got bored,

Well, you left.

There are break-ups and there are heartbreaks

I should have a Ph.D. in knowing the emotions it makes

I've had plenty of break-ups

The kind where it's mutually agreed; no more make-ups

But heartbreaks a different taste

At first thinking, it just needed space

You know, take a moment and climb back into bed

But the pillow sideways keeps me company instead

So, I want to reach out

I might drunk text, any other time I'm too proud

It took 6 months

First 2 with the hope you'd come back

You didn't and I don't know if I can keep up this act

Month 3 and 4 to grieve your touch

Hoping it'd reach you, but no luck

We don't even need to start again I'd settle for a goodbye cuddle

5 & 6 I picked up the broken pieces of our puzzle

6 months of realising you were never meant to fit this picture

6 months of heartbreak and I must be the fixer

6 months of realising you are never coming back

6 months of feeling placed inside a book.

The ghost of you haunts me everyday,

But you're still alive

Maybe it's the stranger in the crowd who smells just like you

The laughter of the happy couple in the supermarket

Or the smell of the food where we had our last date

It all comes back to you

Your ghost still visits me in my dreams

On those days, I don't get out of bed

Those are the days I love the most

Because in my dreams, I'm not haunted by you

I am loved by you.

You don't know my favourite colour anymore

I've changed It

I changed my bedding

It's not dark with cigarette holes

They're brighter and softer with décor pillows

And it smells like fresh cotton

I changed my smell too

Nothing like the earthy wood you liked

But a faint fresh aroma with a hint of cocoa butter

I even got a new phone

And Siri doesn't know your number

I don't know what's more comforting

The fact I don't know you anymore

Or

That you don't know me.

You were my life

Life is all about give and take

I gave you all of me

And you took it

You & I

We're no exception.

When you decided to leave,

Why did you take so much?

There're still parts of me in your suitcase

I never knew you tucked them away

Hid them in between the clothes and bittersweet goodbyes

I searched everywhere,

It's not surprising I couldn't find parts of me since.

Toxic Love

For the closure you deserve.

I now know why storms are named after people

This wasn't your typical love story; no one could have predicted this sequel

It was this love that showed me that love could be evil

Yet it comforted me in a weird way, like enjoying the smell of diesel

I forgive myself for not knowing what I knew then

You're a master of disguise, how could I have seen it was pretend

I believe in your lies and, in solitude, became condemned

But a broken person isn't impossible to mend

And the times I lay thinking about you and the moments I miss

I cast them into the light of your negligence

Reminding myself of the pain and its relevance

You taught me what love wasn't and I have the scars as evidence.

I know what you did

When you told me none of your friends like me

And when you said your mum despised me

I realised that you kept me on a tight leash,

Thinking the world was full of hate,

And only with you, I could be safe

You found tactics in my vulnerable

Left in your silent rage, uncomfortable

Until the authentic me became undiscoverable

Years after you left, I questioned the reality

At first, I wanted you to come back to me

We'd live happily ever after miraculously

Then you spoke badly of me

The lies you told, I couldn't remember

So, *the truth they had to be*

My memory distorted, but in dribs and drabs, it comes back to
me

Now I remember,

Now I know what you did.

I convinced

My friends

My family

Your friends

Your family

My HEART

That we were meant to be together,

But I couldn't convince my own gut feeling

I didn't know why.

Words stain

Because you spue your poison and kiss me straight after

Now the taste lingers like blood

A taste I try to forget, but we all know.

My friends, family and even my therapist tell me to never get
back with you

I think they all assume because of how much you broke me, its
going to be easy

Easy to walk away and not to look back,

That breaking free is a relief

The stormy days of ups and downs you put me through I hated

But I loved the calm after it died down and you said sorry

And the sunny Mondays when we finish the weekend without
arguing

Even the days when you starved me of your love

Because it was the last time I truly felt hunger

Now it's all so numb

No ups and downs, black and whites

Just flat and grey

Why am I craving chaos when all I used to want was peace

Pieces of you in every part of me.

My body refuses to remove you

My tongue won't forget your love language

I can't blame you entirely

I ignored the universe pulling us apart time and time again

I bargained with it for us to stay

Gave up myself for us,

And now my Friends and family miss me

And I… I miss toxicity.

I tried to forget you

I ripped every bit of you out of my smile

I found other names to whisper at night

Built walls around my heart

But the way I loved you was unretrievable

So, my brain reminded me of the quiet moments before I slept

The smile clawed its way out of my mouth anyway

The whisper could never overpower the shouting in my heart

And the walls looked like the aftermath of demolition just at the mention of your name

You're not good for me!

When will I finally get it?

I'd rather be the one who got away

Then to be the one who stayed

I'd rather be the one to haunt you

Then to be the one who holds you

Because

I was the one who didn't go

Love was lost a long time ago

I was the one who held on to every piece

The ghost of us disturbs my peace

Because you always idealise those that never did.

My heart's not in my chest

It's in the rubble of our future home you tore down

Yes, I'm still here

Sad, isn't it?

An empty shell tear-stained cheek

Nothing to show for the years we put into this

Just pure heartache

Were they thinner? Better looking? Had more money?

There must be someone else, if not, then

You really left me.

For weeks after you left, I begged to leave me too

And if you were here

You would have let me.

I tried packing your things

In a bold attempt to send them back to you

Some socks, a shirt, even your half-emptied deodorant

And like a bus, it hit me

How do you put in every compliment?

Return every kiss

I can't put every time I held you in this box

Or unwrite every love note and birthday card

I can't unhear the way my name sounds in your mouth

What do I do with all these little things?

What if I can't put them in the box?

I wanted it to be you

&

You didn't want it to be me.

-The End

It didn't matter how many times you hurt me

I loved you harder after every heartbreak

More faith after every sorry

Believed carelessly after every lie

You showed me love was blind

Oh, how I couldn't see you chipped away at every piece of me

I crumbled in your shadow

And when you slammed the door shut, I blew away into thin air

Like a leaf in autumn torn apart from all it has known

I danced in the wind with leaves,

Floated in muddy puddles that craved your clarity

I was ripped and torn between moving on and wanting you back

But I will find the grass and cling onto it

I will root my self-esteem so deep

Through rain and snow because guess what?

The sun's coming and when it appears, I will grow

I will grow tall and strong, withstanding it all

I will water myself with knowledge, become life's student

When people look at me, they will admire my strength

I'll be that tree that still has one leaf all winter

Because I refuse to lose all of me again.

I told myself; love should feel like this

Like a smooth whiskey

Until you've had one glass to many

Next thing you know, you're lying on the bathroom floor

The world is spinning, nothing in this chaos makes sense

I need to purge, get you out of my system

But I won't let it go

I swallow it down painfully

Behave how I was taught to

Can't recognise anything about the love I once knew

When the dust settles, you'll be there again

But only to pour another glass

Maybe this time, wiping away my tears

Or I could do it—I chose this

Brought me to my knees, but I drank it away

It feels like home

And I've always been a homebody.

Patient Love

For all the love that will take

some time.

I want to love you

So bad

But I hope you know loving you will take time

Not because you aren't worthy of all the love this world could give

But because loving you scares the shit out of me

Because the last time I loved someone the way I want to love you, I almost didn't survive

I don't want you to think it has anything to do with you

Because you are perfect

You're loving and kind

You are everything they weren't

I've never felt so at home like I do whenever you look at me

You take every insecurity

Every anxiety, every hesitation

And put it in your back pocket

And tell me it'll be okay

I wish I knew how you do that

How your touch is the first that didn't make me tremble

Your hands are the first I never want to let go of

Your voice I never wanted to stop hearing

You woke me up like the most beautiful ambient sunrise

So please be patient with me,

I really want to love you.

If I told you I've never been home

Would you trust me enough to take you to ours?

We can sit in a little glass conservatory and watch the stars

A vulnerable space where I could show you all my scars

Isn't it almost *romantic?*

You know….

How fragile I must be, like glass

Unseen and unheard, someone the world looks past

Never really a part of a home.

Just something to add value to the bricks I'm attached to

And the way you'll save me

It'll almost be *poetic*

But

What if I saved myself?

And the value of these bricks turned to dust

What if I made my exterior so beautiful?

Would people travel to spend time with me like they stay in glass igloos & watch the northern lights?

What if, like Kew Gardens, I promise to give them butterflies? Would they stay?

If I could change their views instead of visiting the Shard

Then would the shards of emptiness cut less?

I'd stop bleeding; the reasons you should stay.

Sync up with me

When the timing is right

11.11

I know you've been broken

Letting someone in is far too scary; it's often hard to stay open

You search for evidence they don't love you

But love is at the core of everything they do

That little thing they brought because you crossed their mind

Running a bath, lighting a candle or two to help you unwind

After a hard day's work ordering your favourite takeaway

Saying yes to eating something small from their plate

Just take a breath and look around

See the love that you've found

Sometimes actions speak louder than words

And I LOVE YOU doesn't always have to be conversed.

How did you find me?

I wasn't trying to be found

I spent so long in the air and only put my two feet on the ground

I've taken a few steps and still learning to walk

The path ahead of me is like no other I've trodden before

The grounds are uneven and my feet are sore

There are still days I don't know if I can go on anymore

And yet, in this crowded place, our eyes meet

Before a chance, you're at my feet

I went to speak but was too much in my head

I went to sleep with you in my head

Everything I want to keep walks out instead

My mind was nothing like I've ever known, but I'd call it a beautiful mess

A person like no other, who has my interest

As days pass, I'm learning more

If I didn't know any better, I'd say I knew you before

It's all so new but familiar on this tour

My glass is half empty, but you're willing to pour.

I can't trust you to love me the way I deserve

But I want to.

I want to share with you

All the places that make me,

Me!

I'd take you to where

I had my heartbreak, my first kiss,

My favourite place to watch the stars

The quiet place, I watch the sunrise

And the water I sit to cry by when I'm sad

I want to take you to the parts of me I call home

Welcome you in

And if you like it, stay a while.

They told me I was too young to give up on love

And they were right

Heartbreak from my teenage love left me pessimistic

Had me so cautious I could only play it safe

You held my hand and said let's sit here on the ledge

Made my heart soft and kept my boundaries strong

The summer days we spent warm side by side

I followed your essence with confidence back to the ledge

We'd sit some more

When I wasn't with you, thoughts of you were never far

I never knew I could feel this way

You created a safe space for me between falling and being firmly on the ground

I feel safe enough to walk off the ledge with you

I trust you wouldn't lead into danger

I'm ready to fall

Meet me at the ledge.

I love the way you carry your heart

Dream of a life less confusing

How you hope for better things

You strive to do the best with all that you do

And

The little things we can't agree you love me through the
difference

When I nccd direction, your words are like a compass

You took me out of survival mode and showed me to live

Let me know that my best was safe with you

My love for you exists in every atom of the moments we share

Until I'm ready, will you carry my heart too?

I can still remember my heart pounding in my chest

From the inside, it sounded like a hammer against cloth

Every blood vessel around my lungs felt as if they would explode

My legs couldn't bare the weight of the anticipation

You wrapped your arms around me

Placed your hand behind my ear

And just like that

I felt the calm of the Atlantic.

The day we met was just an ordinary day

No romantic spark or butterflies under the night sky

I didn't even think much of it

I've met so many people in this lifetime

That woman, when I was waiting for the bus

Even asked a taxi driver how his day was

But I do remember seeing you again

How my eyes wouldn't stop lingering on your face

I had a feeling you'd become someone important

I've never been a *"written in the stars"* type

Maybe my heart knew before my head

This beautiful coincidence on such an ordinary day

Maybe now I believe in destiny.

When you choose me, I want it to be effortless

I know it sounds silly but,

Out of a million beautiful things, I was drawn to you.

I pray that you don't leave because I'm not always blooming

I will open up when I'm ready; please be patient

I always face the sun; it keeps me happy and able to grow

I know there are a million amazing people around me, but
you've still got to pick me

My roots are so deep in the stance I refuse to be unearthed for
another;

Another who just wants to cut me, contain me in a vase and
throw me away when I'm not blooming.

My love will always be unmatched

If you decide it's me

I don't need a fancy place to live in

Just keep me by the rays of your love.

We will grow deeper together

Roots so entwined no storm could rip us from the ground

If they tried and succeeded, we'd still be holding onto each
other.

Would it be okay, if I loved you in solitude?

While you carry out daily tasks

The kinda love you can feel and know,

I just haven't announced it yet,

I know it's a little selfish; I just don't want the world to know

See, I've told the world I don't believe anymore

So,

You're detrimental to this self-proclaimed image

I don't know if the world is ready to see me like this.

Love is stupid!

That's what I used to say

Until I met you;

You have a hold on my heart that I couldn't brake if I tried

And believe me, in moments of fear, I have wanted to.

This journey has been humbling and painful at times

It's been long and trying, but we are still trying

Everyday you decide to keep getting up and being open

I came to terms with the fact love is stupid

It's never made any sense

With you, it doesn't have to

I couldn't stop loving you anymore then I could stop breathing

And that still doesn't make sense to me, either.

But I'm learning to be okay with it

I love you beyond what you or I could imagine

If I was no longer here, my love would reach you in whispers of
the wind

My love is unbound by time or space

It will always exist.

Healing
Love

for the love that hugs your

soul.

In life, I have everything to lose, but you

Loving you

It was late, say 2 AM

You shuddered the cold breeze

Turned with your back to me

Tactfully,

I put my arms around you, bringing you back to me

I got up, closed the window, shut the curtain,

Kissed you softly on your forehead

Just like that, I knew for certain

I have nothing to lose by loving you

Like a defiant teenager, my heart stopped listening to me and listened to you instead

I decided to climb Mount Everest in your head

Trying to peak at your soul, but got too close to the edge

And then…

I fell in love

Like burning lava straight from the depths of your core chasing me

I mean HOT lava overwhelming, melting, embracing me

Burned down every wall facing me

A fire that SCREAMS

Just let me love you

Making it hard for me to breathe,

But please stay close to me

I might cut you with shards of fear

But please stay close to me,

When I move, move with me

Let me inhale your every exhale

I fell for you,

Remember,

I fell for you.

All the sunsets

&

Sunrises,

The full moon,

And all these stars

Yet,

You still choose to stare at me.

The way love has made me travel for miles,

The way love has made me fall and hurt,

The way love has broken me,

The way love has pushed and crossed my boundaries,

The way love kept my belly empty when I was lovesick,

And the way love left me sleepless at night.

The way love did all this

Nothing like the love I now know

Love with you is so effortless and simple.

Have you ever stepped outside into the sun?

That moment where your eyes have no choice but to squint shut

You feel warmth wrap around every piece of exposed flesh

A deep breath to inhale the warmth

Allowing the sun to touch your heart, lungs and soul.

The breeze passes your face,

Reminding you to exhale slowly.

A chirping bird from afar the whispers

Open your eyes,

The world looks so much more colourful

And you feel so at ease

Is this what love feels like?

Cause if it is,

You are my sunshine, my only sunshine.

I find myself staring,

Thinking of you,

I fell so deeply in love the first time I saw you,

And if I lost my memory today, I could wake up tomorrow,

Meet you all over again and fall in love with no hesitation.

I want

No, no, no…

I NEED you to know how much I love you

Whilst I lay here reading, thinking of you.

I wish I could articulate the way I feel

If I could just explain the feeling when I hear your name in a crowd

Or the warmth when I wake up greeted by your face

I wish you knew how I describe you to strangers

And all the songs on the radio that remind me of you

The lyrics of these love songs are true, but they don't quite give you enough justice

You came into my life a hero with no cape

Someone my inner child needed to meet

You;

You healed parts of me I never knew hurt

I wish I knew how to say thank you.

Let's make mistakes together

We're not supposed to know how to do things we've never done before.

-A healthy relationship

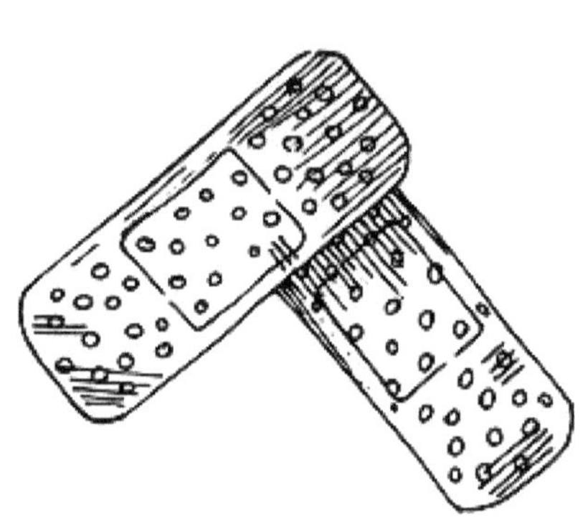

I know I'm good for your ego, but I'll still tell you the truth even if it hurts,

And if I tell you to handle me with intention, it's because I love me first

You could try loving me better and our love will excel in expectation

We could materialise every dream beyond imagination

See our love organically grow your maturity

And this exchange of words, my heart in my throat, provides you security,

Something you never knew existed

Making you regret the time spent resisting

Open your mind, soul and heart feel this love is real

The kind of love that can do all and

Heal.

I feel guilty whenever you compliment me

Because I don't believe you

And I hate to think of you in such a way

As if you'd really say things untrue

It's not in your nature, I believe you

I love YOU enough to want to love myself too.

I overthink so much,

You over-explain more

My anxieties are worst at night,

You let me fall asleep first

I get hangry a lot after a long day,

You ask me what I want to eat before asking how my day was

Receiving gifts can make me feel awkward,

You give me memories and butterflies instead

I'm indecisive when we go out for food,

You order something different, so I can have a taste of both

I tell you, I *"need"* to be alone when I'm falling apart,

You hold me close and put me back together again

Getting out of bed is hard some days,

You keep me warm in the covers until I'm ready

I asked for adjectives of how much you love me,

You gave me verbs.

I am cautious to bear that of another soul

For if others saw me fully exposed

They wouldn't love me like they claimed to

Time & experience have taught me to trust no one

Friends, lovers and family had betrayed me all until you

I am reckless, selfish, stubborn and sometimes rude

Just bottled-up emotions of a heart that was broken too soon

Please forgive me.

Maybe I'll write about you,

And all the things that remind me of how safe you make me feel

I'd list all the memoirs that greet me

Like how we share clothes and I smell them before I put them to wash

Your toothbrush, I put back in the holder after you leave

Add your songs to my playlist and imagine how you feel listening to them

How I stay up late watching movies with characters that remind me of you

The time I bought a jumper because it was the same colour as your eyes

My phone even brings up our photos to remind me how happy we are

A dandelion that bursts in the breath of my wish

And all the dispersed seeds, these memoirs

They all lead back to you.

I love you like I love the woods,

Whether the trees are bare or full

The way you deserved to be loved

In every season,

I love you like the waves of the sea,

Whether the tide is high or low

The way you deserved to be loved

Rough tides and times don't last forever

I love you like a junk draw,

Whether it's difficult to open or not

The way you deserved to be loved

You'll always have the tools when I need them most

I love you,

In all that you are and grow to be

The way you deserved to be loved

Unconditionally.

You came into my life and changed everything

Your love is unmatched

Raised my standard to a level I knew existed outside of movies

You make me laugh, a proper belly laugh,

I feel like myself more than ever since the day we met

The way you are is something so beautiful I couldn't find the words to truly describe it

All I know is it brings a certain peace that I crave when I'm alone

I'm terrified to lose you

There is no one like you on this earth

Someone warm and soft

Polite and thoughtful

Everyone deserves someone like you.

Stay Love

for the love that we deserve

mutually.

I like the way we feel together

We just fit

I've never fit with someone like we do

Handcrafted somewhere in time and space

To indefinitely be with each other

Please let it last forever

If we ever broke apart

We could always come back and fit again

Because the same part of me would break too

So we will always fit.

I'm too intense for coffee or drinks

I love movies, but from the comfort of home

Anxiety kicks my butt often, but I'm intrinsically a social butterfly

I'm trying to understand how I'm such a contradiction

A good listener too, tell me your dreams

We can talk all night until one of us falls asleep

I fall in love immediately or not at all

So, we should get married

Not because we crossed paths by chance

But because since you stopped, life hasn't been the same

And I fell,

Immediately.

You have decided to love all of me

In the same way, someone decides to get up every morning

Even go to work everyday

Or decides to watch a movie to the end

Thank you.

In the days of grey

I see a cover of a book that I know in my soul could be the one I was yearning to read

The one I'd pay attention to when it speaks

And if it dares say

"I love you"

I'd believe

Asked all the right questions to get a taste of the writing on each page

Maybe this book could explain how fairy tales were made

I searched through crowds till I found you on the bottom shelf

Your delicate spine in my hands, I know I trust myself

This familiar heat in my belly reminds me we both walked through hell

But the heat never burns

And my stomach doesn't churn

No matter how many pages I turn

Your love, I've come to learn.

Meeting you happened by chance

Destiny,

Fate, if you will

The only way to describe it…

It was like listening to my favourite song, not knowing it would be my favourite

Now I know all the lyrics, every beat and hum the melody

No matter how many times I listen to it, it'll still bring me back to that very first

This song sees me in the raw when I have my headphones on, shut off from the world

I felt like driving for hours with the radio playing full volume on repeat

It's a timeless R&B song

A slow classic

A whimsical piece by Beethoven

In all that it is

It's you.

Do you think the birds that sit outside our widow know you're away

Do you think they miss you or know that I miss you,

And they gather to keep each other company or for me

The birds cawk and sing until your return

Like me singing sad songs until the hours before you arrive home

You walk through the door and sing with me, my songbird

Tell me you love me, my love bird

Put on something comfy let's nest in watching Netflix

Oh, how I love you, little bird.

I look at our photograph

Remembering that very moment and all that it captured

The music that was playing in the background

The smell of your clothes as you leaned into me

Although we were frozen in time, I can still remember the
moments that followed

And the moments that came just before

This beautiful display of us

A time capsule masterpiece

I hope my eyes are open; I don't want to miss a thing.

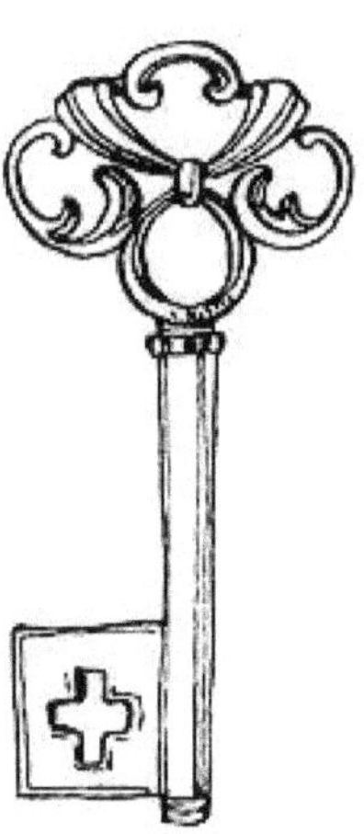

Maybe I'll forgive you

And in turn, I'll forgive myself too

I owe that to me

I'll learn the secret of how one becomes WE

I won't run from these butterflies instead, I'll believe

My heart's a compass; I'm blinded I'll use it to see

And then maybe,

Just maybe

The person that comes to mind they do have the key.

Imagine I wrote about you?

Like

Before I even met you

Every curve, crease, your touch and peace;

These aren't just written words

This is a wish

Wish you were here already.

-A lonely Soul

If you want forever

I'll take the batteries out of my clock

I will pause this very moment

You can be infinitely mine

And if one of us dies,

I'll put the batteries back

So I could watch the seconds count down

Until we meet again.

The way you love me

I could only be consumed with ecstasy at the thought of you

The smell of shea butter,

The pout just before you laugh or smile,

And just how beautiful it is to miss you

Because it confirms our love is real

Oh, how everything fell into place

When you fell into my arms

I know for certain

If I had never met you,

I would permanently feel like something's missing.

Until I met you,

I didn't know I was over my ex

I believed I'd never get them out of my mind

Until I met you,

It was the longest relationship I'd ever had

I was sure I could never find something that intense

Until I met you,

Countless nights I lost sleep

I thought I'd messed up the only shot I had at love

Until I met you,

I don't even remember their favourite colour

But I know yours

Something I didn't think was possible

Until I met you,

You taught me how to forget

And start over, be loved and love again

Thank you… but I don't want to do that again

I don't want to face forgetting you.

Do you believe in love at first sight?

I'm not sure I do,

But I know I love you

And I feel as though I always have

I don't remember my love for you growing day by day

It's just a surge of emotion that takes over me

Come to think of it

When I look back at the day I met you

And I remember seeing your face for the first time

I can't help but feel that same rush of love come over me

So maybe it's true

Maybe I always did love you from first sight

I just never knew.

I want the clichés with you

Make me a playlist with all the songs that remind me of you

Let me forget my clothes on your bedroom floor

I want to swing arms when we hold hands walking down the
street

Can we go to the movies and put our arms around each other?

I want it all with you

In turn, you're the cliché that I want

Say you want it too?

Tick

Yes   or   No